PRESENTED TO:

_____

FROM:

_____

Shine!

Carrying My Father's Light

Author: Kimberly Trembly-Carr

Editor: Emily Pogue
Cover artwork by: Zybrena Porter (www.zybrena.com)

Dedication

This book is lovingly dedicated to my brother, Scott Trembly.

I promised Dad that I would tell you, and somehow make you believe, all the things he was trying to tell you; but you couldn't hear.

You are so loved, Scott.

No matter what you think you've done, or how unlovable you believe you are... You are worthy of great love.

Dad loved you… so very very much. As do I, more than you could ever know.

Foreword

Hi. My name is Kimberly, and I am ordinary.

Sounds just a little bit like a confession from a 12-Step Meeting, doesn't it?

You can't see the ridiculous grin on my face right now, but I think maybe there should be a group meeting for excessively ordinary people!

I'm not just a little bit ordinary.

No. No. No.

I'm the cliché plain Jane, girl-next-door kind of ordinary.

I tell you that because if you're going to read this, it wouldn't be enjoyable or authentic without knowing who I am first.

I promise you. I am not extraordinary!

So, who am I?

As far as I know, I'm not the envy of other moms. If I am, I have no idea why. I may be the mom the others are talking about under their breath!

I have three beautiful boys of my own, one stepson I work hard to get along with daily, and an estranged stepdaughter that, unfortunately, I barely know. I also have two other children I love as my own, although they are no longer mine through marriage.

My husband and I have each been married two times before (we are ridiculously flawed), but we suppose the third time's the charm.

Or maybe it's because there is a different element, a spiritual element, involved this time around.

I believe my husband is an incredible man who is irritatingly smart and has an enormous heart. He is driven, stubborn, and entirely perfect for me. Somehow, he loves me like nobody's business. While I'm very blessed to have him, I get a bit nervous introducing him to strangers. He's one of those guys you either really like or you really don't. He lets you form your own opinions and isn't bothered by them.

Because of his help, I've been able to work from home. While I don't consider myself a writer, penning a book has always been something I've dreamed of doing. I think it's like singing in the shower versus singing on stage, a gigantic leap. Even though I didn't think anyone would want to read what I had to say, there was something inside of me that wouldn't let go of the idea.

This book was the whisper that wouldn't go away. It was something a beloved Deacon at my church asked me to do following the death of my hero, my first love, my father, Delford Trembly.

That Deacon wanted me to preserve (in writing) the life-giving details of what my father shared with me during the last week we spent together before he passed away.

I spent months trying to write this book but could just not find the words.

That changed when I went to a women's conference at my church. At that gathering, I heard words of empowerment that only reaffirmed my conviction to write.

I realized that this wasn't just about the details of the most painful suffering and separation I've ever experienced; this was going to be much more. After years of reflection and examination, I realized there is a message here I must share.

I'm sure that you've noticed I've mentioned church a couple of times.

Oh no!

Yes, I am a Jesus follower.

Some of you may be thinking, "Whoopie! Good for you! Me, too. It's not that big of a deal." For others, it might be a bit more, "Great! She's going to preach through the whole book," as your eyes roll to the back of your head.

I promise, I won't…

I am going to tell you stories that can relate to scripture, stories that show you what I believe are miracles. Stories that shine a bright light on all the dark places in your life, so that you can start to find the missing pieces of your own great big puzzle! (If your puzzle is already complete, you must contact me immediately!)

As you work your way through this book, I encourage you to consider how all *your* struggles and tragedies could be part of something bigger. Allow them to have a more significant and more positive meaning in your life. Give yourself the chance, if only while you read this book, to look at your troubles in a new light.

My true intention is to help you find hope, whether it is freshly cultivated or simply renewed. I wish you hope to have enough faith to see your life in a different light.

If you want to label me as "Christian," I will accept it. Christian is a beautifully descriptive word. To me, "Christian" means to be Christ like. Christ was compassionate, loving, forgiving, accepting of all people, and He was full of peace. I am simply fine with any of those labels.

I hope to show you the meaning of "Christian" through this book. Therefore, I ask that you read on with an open heart. Allow me to bring you love and light, hope and faith to cast out your fear. If I can help you do that, in my opinion, that's Christian.

Lastly, you should know that every story is my own and not a work of fiction. I have tried to share each story to the best of my recollection and in full transparency.

While I can't say for sure why everything has happened the way it has, my faith would help me answer that all things are working together for a greater good.

I think *you* are the "good", and you need this.

Just believe.

Anyone, even an extremely "plain-Jane" ordinary person like myself, can experience extraordinary miracles.

You are just as unique.

Be light,
Kim

Table of Contents

Dedication   v
Foreword   vii
Chapter 1: The Light Giver   1
Chapter 2: My First Miracle   7
Chapter 3: The Struggle is Real   21
Chapter 4: Wave after Wave   29
Chapter 5: You'll want to come to church   37
Chapter 6: Internal Surgery   43
Chapter 7: The Line   49
Chapter 8: Broken   57
Chapter 9: Twenty-six   67
Chapter 10: One-hundred-seventy-eight   79
Chapter 11: Going Home   89
Epilogue   99
About the Author   105

*"Declare his glory among the nations,
his marvelous deeds among all peoples."
1 Chronicles 16:24- New International Version (NIV)*

Chapter 1: The Light Giver

"In the same way, let your light shine before others, that they may see your good deeds and glorify your Father in heaven."
Matthew 5:16- New International Version (NIV)

I watched the Sunday School Teacher as she turned her back and went to put a tub of toys up on a shelf. I'd spent the entire time in the nursery that day playing with a little plastic lamb.

It was a perfect representation of the lamb you'd imagine in nursery stories, and I was in love with it. At just three years old, it barely fit in my palm. As the teacher turned her back, I sneakily put the little guy into my tiny pocket. I had every intention of continuing to play with the little lamb at home.

Later, my daddy found me playing with the lamb and asked, "Kim, where did you get that?"

I told him how much I loved the little lamb, how that little lamb and I had bonded over several nursery days while he and momma had attended church service. I explained how the little lamb needed to come home with me to play until the next nursery day at church.

My daddy didn't get mad. Instead, he used that little embarrassment as the first of several opportunities to teach his daughter a lesson. He marched my little butt, with tear-glistened cheeks, right back to the church nursery.

As we walked back to the church, he told me how God felt about my actions. He told me what I'd done was stealing and that the lamb was the church's lamb, not my lamb.

He told me that while he was disappointed in my choice and that God was too, they both still loved me. Then he explained that I wasn't allowed to be selfish and keep him as my own; he belonged to the nursery.

As the years have drawn on, I look back on that day with fond memory. Despite my childish choice, I am awestruck at how amazing my dad was for using that opportunity to teach me something I would never, ever forget.

It was the first time I would see my father shine! He built me up when he could've filled me with fear. I'm blessed to say it was just the beginning. He became exceptionally skilled at this as he grew older.

He became a beacon on a hill, shining for all to see. He would share his happiness with anyone who asked, and sometimes those who didn't. He put his faith in God and tried to help as many people as he could by shining light into their world. Others called him Delford or Mr. Trembly, but I called him my daddy, my inspiration.

Most of this story will be about him. He was a large part of my day-to-day and the main character in some significant events of my life; both in the mundane and in the great big. He was one of my biggest fans and remains my hero.

Who was my dad?

He grew up as one of four children in a very rural Nebraska town in the forties. His hometown was the kind of place that most people wouldn't have given a second thought to as they briefly drove through. He would often tell stories of sleeping on an ironing board and eating meals of only bread and water. He was a proud Veteran, a Scoutmaster in Boy Scouts, and a respected Business Manager. He loved all things outdoors, including fishing and gardening. And oh, how he loved kids; his and everyone else's.

In 2005 he retired.

Well, not entirely. I say that because for the 18 months following that 'retirement,' my dad lovingly took on the role of 'nanny' for my twin boys. He'd wanted twins since he had grown up caring for his twin cousins. I was blessed to bring another set of "Trembly Twins" into the world.

I'm so grateful I had him to leave my little people with, and he was an amazing caretaker.

Dad believed in the bible. We went to church throughout the majority of my childhood. I grew up in a household where religion wasn't something everyone talked about daily, but the bible was something I knew we believed in.

In the last four years of his life, my dad became a Sunday School teacher. Ironically, his last few visits to our church weren't to teach the children but instead were spent learning how to better use the talents that God had bestowed upon him.

Although he wasn't able to sit through the entire service on his final visit to church, he did get to see his four grandsons baptized. He was so proud. He pounded his cane on the ground, smiled at me, and said: "Well, that's one of my prayers answered!"

My dad was amazing. Everyone who met him loved him; good people, bad people, lost people, found people, all people.

He never preached. He had a way of making you feel comfortable enough that you'd soon find yourself sharing your deepest secrets. My father's goal was to keep people from being lonely and hopeless. Those interactions made a difference in the everyday lives of so many people.

My father left this earthly world on July 28, 2018, and just how impactful he had become was evident. At his funeral, there were people I had never met; people I never knew that he even knew. They came to share their stories and pay respect to a man who had been their light.

An American Indian woman sang a Native Song of Passage over my father at his viewing. She explained my father had taught her daughter to read, kept her son out of a gang, and had often sat with her at home.

There was a man who said that he had shared a monthly breakfast with my father, who laughed and cried. He hugged me and said that my father was his 'joy.'

There was another man, about my age, who said that my father had taught him everything he knew about being a father and the importance of family. He shared, "He loved you. He was proud of you, and he thought you were so strong".

Who were these people? Where was I when he was making friends of them? No one arrived to proclaim that my dad had taught them about the bible. No one rose and said that my father was a great preacher. There wasn't one person that announced my father was a fantastic Christian.

To them, he was love.
To them, he was the brightest light.
To them, he was Christ-like.

That is a noble accomplishment, and a goal I now strive for daily. I want to be light.

Chapter 2: My First Miracle

*"He replied, "Because you have so little faith. Truly I tell
you, if you have faith as small as a mustard seed, you can
say to this mountain, 'Move from here to there,' and it will
move.*
Nothing will be impossible for you."
Matthew 17:20- New International Version (NIV)

$\mathcal{B}$efore I can tell you about the miracle I experienced
with my father, I need to walk you through my very first
miracle.

I met my first husband through work, and we married when I was 25. After two years of living the newlywed life, we agreed to settle down and start a family. Soon, I was pregnant and nervous. The thought of being a mom frightened me.

At the beginning of my pregnancy, I developed placenta previa, which is a condition where the placenta that feeds the baby, is blocking the outlet to the uterus called the cervix. Although it can cause bleeding throughout pregnancy and during delivery, the doctor assured me it was quite common and that with time, everything was going to be okay.

As my pregnancy progressed, I felt more and more anxious. My then-husband was concerned about becoming a father, as well. Unfortunately, he lessened his anxiety by increasing his trips to the local pub. His absence made my anxiety all the worse. My blood pressure and swelling slowly became out of control.

My doctor agreed to induce my labor three weeks earlier than my due date because of my inability to keep my blood pressure under control. With our bag packed and car seat loaded, we were off to meet our little boy or girl. We were so excited for the surprise!

I had a dose of Pitocin to help get my labor started. Despite the medication and all the walking, there was no difference; this baby was quite simply not going to follow our plan. Six hours in, our doctor instructed the nurses to break my waters. While it was something that they often do to accelerate labor, it hurt so badly! I cried and turned to my mother, who had been worriedly staying by my side. They gave me another round of Pitocin, and we waited.

After 24 hours, I was exhausted. Nothing was happening. The nurses recommended I have an epidural that would give me a break and allow me to sleep. They said that the epidural would help alleviate the pain of the contractions. I tried to explain that I hadn't felt any yet.

Although I hadn't felt any contractions, the nurses assured me that I had had them. They explained that the monitor that read my baby's heartbeat had shown a few dips at regular intervals that suggested I had been contracting. With their confidence that things were progressing normally, I accepted the epidural, and sleep came.

I'm not sure how long I rested. In what felt like minutes, I awakened from a kick by my baby that was stronger than any kick I'd felt before. At that same moment, the monitor beeped as my baby's heart rate flat-lined. Startled, I yelled for the nurses.

By the time they arrived, the baby's heartbeat had faintly returned. The nurses believed I imagined the kick, but I knew there was something wrong. I just knew it. Looking back, I have no idea how I could've known. It was merely a whisper, a nudge. Call it a mother's intuition.

I all but demanded a Cesarean Section at that point. The nurses agreed to call the doctor but said that he wouldn't be happy about it. Gathering my strength, I demanded they perform a C-Section, and within the hour, I prepped for surgery. We both entered the operating room with fear.

After strapping me onto the table and checking to ensure the epidural would continue to work, my doctor arrived. His irritation was palpable, and as he checked my dilation one last time, he seemed even more disappointed in his findings.

"Well, if you want a C-Section and you just can't wait, I'll do it. I think it's a bit too soon to call, but…" my Doctor stated.

I laughed, nearly hysterical. I explained that I knew, at my core, that there was something wrong and because the doctor was the only one skilled enough to get the baby out to fix what was wrong, we needed to do it. Although I honestly doubt he believed me, he prepped for surgery.

My child's father watched squeamishly and with worry as they precisely made the incisions. My preoccupation with the baby's condition overshadowed any anxiety I was feeling.

At last, they announced they could see the baby. It was time for the big reveal!

"Kimmie, it's a boy!" My child's father was overjoyed.

"Yes, he is," said the doctor. "A great BIG boy! Dad, would you like to do the honor and cut the cord?"

As my son's father cut his umbilical cord, our whole world changed.

Almost instantly, the baby's coloring went from a healthy pinkish hue to a purple-black color. Everyone in the room abandoned what they were doing and began attending to the little boy to whom I had just given birth. My little boy was placed on the crash cart, and life- saving efforts started. I anxiously watched as they began heart palpitations and pushed air into his lungs with a small bag over his tiny nose. Hurriedly, they rushed our boy away from us, past his grandparents waiting in the hall, and off to save his life.

My doctor returned to the operating table and quietly finished my surgery, apologizing for the unknown. I was speechless. I could do nothing but cry. My son's father looked at me with fear in his eyes. I told him to go; to find our son. Despite the doctor's reassurances, he needed to go find out what was happening.

In what felt like hours later, I went into a recovery room. It was here that my doctor joined us, holding a printout of my baby's heartbeat from the monitor. Through shock and tears, he admitted that he had no idea what had happened. He assured me he would find out exactly what went wrong.

Meanwhile, in the Neonatal Intensive Care Unit (NICU), my nearly ten-pound baby boy topped the charts for weight. Babies born this early are not usually so big. Most often, larger babies that are born prematurely have only minor issues. Our child filled an incubator from head to toe. He was not breathing on his own and couldn't regulate his blood pressure. The APGAR test administered to newborns, measures their appearance, pulse, grimace, activity, and respiration. Each of those five factors is given a rating from 0, being worst, to 2, being best. A completely healthy baby would score between 7-10. Our baby scored a "1".

The next morning, the doctor returned to my room, where he quietly explained he believed he had discovered the problem. The placenta previa I had did not correct itself as expected. When the nurse broke my bag of waters, she poked a hole in the placenta, which then bled into the amniotic fluid. As a result, my child had spent the greater part of 21 hours breathing blood into his little lungs. Because of this, he had developed very severe pneumonia in utero.

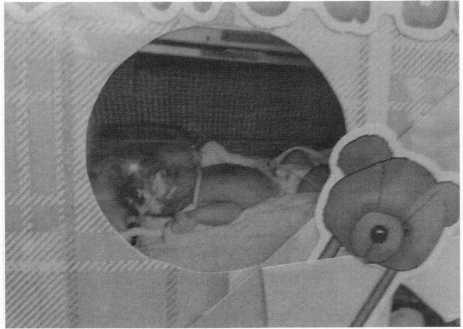

A meeting with the Neonatologist gave us an x-ray view of our son's tiny lungs and a bleak outlook. His doctors allowed me to see him through the glass of the isolate. Because my voice excited him and made his blood pressure erratic, I wasn't able to talk to him. His eyes were taped shut. Life providing tubes came out of the top of his head, his arms, his legs, and his nose.

I cried and cried. I was powerless. I kept wondering if I was going to lose him; this child I'd never even had the chance to hold... I can remember thinking that he had never seen me. He would never even know I was there with him.

That Monday evening, the doctors again came to my room. They explained how every child gets the "right-to-thrive" per hospital and ethical policy. It means that if a child wouldn't have the ability to sustain life on its own, their system said that it wasn't our place or within our power to keep that child alive. They had come to tell me that they were going to be removing the tube that was putting breath into my son at 1:00 a.m. It would be left to my newborn son to fight for his own life.

My head was reeling. I was given the opportunity to see my son one last time that evening. I stood before his isolate and promised him I'd be the best mother ever if he'd just give me a chance. I told him how I'd prepared, read all about babies, and had everything ready for his homecoming. I promised to protect him and love him unconditionally. I begged him to want to come home with me. I stayed so long before his incubator that the nurses had to take me away. While he never saw me with his eyes, I prayed he had heard me with his heart.

With a broken spirit, I returned to my room, which now felt like a prison cell; cold and hopeless. While my son's father paced the halls of the hospital to cope, I handled things a bit differently. I called everyone I knew. They were all so excited to hear from me as they had known we'd headed to the hospital. Many of them joyously asked about the baby and when they would be able to see us.

With a heavy heart and a lump in my throat, I repeatedly explained to each person what was happening. Just as I'd begged my son, I begged my friends to keep my son in their thoughts and prayers. I pleaded to them that they raise prayers for healing. Those who truly loved me, I believed, would remember my son as they went to sleep. More than visits, cards, or flowers, I reminded them I needed them to pray.

My mother and father never left my side. They watched with concern as I broke down. Others described me as a strong person. I believed in God and had faith, but I also thought I wasn't good enough to be a mom. I thought I wasn't worthy of receiving blessings. I believed the lies inside my head that said I had done so many horrible things in this life, and was such a disappointment, that God wouldn't want me to have such a blessing as this child. If I were honest with myself, I'd felt that way my entire pregnancy. After all, children belong to God and are only ours to steward over for a short while. I believed I was such a mess; how could God entrust a baby to me? How could He believe in me? Would I believe in me?

Having just had surgery, the nurses prompted me to walk. Despite standing by my child's side for so long, I had now been sitting in bed with little movement for hours. So, I got up and walked with my father.

Side-by-side, we walked along the catwalk that ran above the lobby area of the hospital. We mindlessly and silently circled it like a track. Most of the time, I was trembling from tears. My father and I stopped just outside my room to gaze over the people coming and going from the gift shop below. I was still crying.

Finally, my dad took a deep breath, squeezed my hand, and said: "You know, honey, he's going to be okay."

I tearfully said, "I hope so."

"I know so." My father responded in a solid and comforting tone he had used many times before.

"How do you know so?" I asked him.

With a small grin, my father pointed up. I shook my head in disbelief as my dad started to explain, "I know he will be okay because He told me."

I curiously asked how He had told him to which my father replied, "He just did, and I heard Him. I wish you wouldn't worry so much."

I told my father that I wished I had his faith.

Back in my room, one of my girlfriends called to see how I was doing. She wanted me to know that she'd taken our talk earlier in the day seriously. She'd reached out to her in-laws who were devout in faith, and they had organized a candlelight vigil for 8:00 p.m. that evening. Additionally, she and her family and several of their church's members were setting their alarms to 1:00 a.m. to start praying. I felt so grateful. The thought that she had done so much in such a short time for my little boy touched me.

When I informed my in-laws of this great gift, my girlfriend and her church family were giving to us through prayer, they were not as gracious. While fear had propelled me to look for hope and walk in faith through prayer, fear had caused them to be angry; angry that, in their eyes, God was trying to take their only grandchild from them. Instead of praying, they were cursing God. My child's father was angry, too, and said that he didn't have the words or want to pray. We were all just so scared.

I fell asleep that night listening to the music I had played for my baby while he was in utero. I prayed my prayers and bargained with God. I told him all the ways I would change and be better if he'd just let me be a mom. I made these promises until exhaustion took over, and I succumbed to sleep.

At 5:00 a.m., the NICU nurse burst through the door to my room where we were all sleeping, some upright in chairs.

"It's a GOOD MORNING! Get up! Get up! Would you like to hold your baby?" she had asked.

"I can hold him? He's well?" I asked in disbelief.

"He's so much better! Come and see the doctor, he'll explain," she replied enthusiastically.

I hurriedly put on my robe and slippers and rushed down the hall with the nurse.

"It's a bit of a miracle actually," She beamed. "I've never seen anything like it."

As we rounded the corner into the NICU, the nurse introduced us to the neonatologist.

"Your boy is really a bit of a mystery," he said as he scratched his head. "We can't explain how he has gotten so well so quickly. This was your baby's lungs yesterday. These are your child's lungs today." He pointed at one x-ray, which showed small black lungs and another that showed tiny white lungs.

It was as if he'd never had pneumonia. They explained my baby was now keeping his blood pressure up without assistance. As they began removing the wires, we rejoiced! We were even happier that if he started to eat well, we could all go home together tomorrow! Then the nurse led me to sit in a chair. She placed my son in my arms, and I wept.

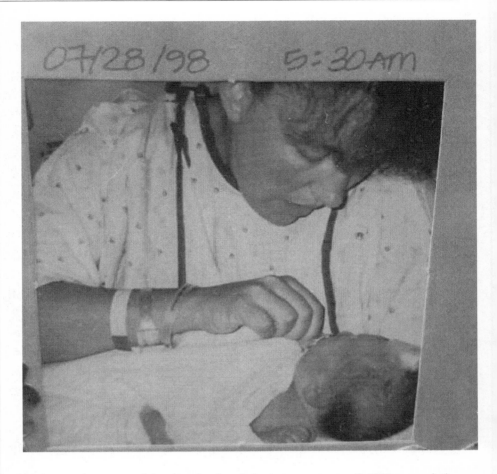

All the tubes on his body had been removed. The quick-connect ends for the IV and wires remained in the top of his head but were invisible to me. He was so fragile and beautiful. Through the tears, I quietly choked out, "Hi, baby." My child opened his eyes and looked up at me. It was then that I understood. That's when I first experienced unconditional love from the perspective of a parent. It is one thing to be loved unconditionally. It is quite another to do the verb and be the one to love unconditionally.

It was the first time I witnessed the genuine power of prayer.

It was the first time I experienced unshakable faith.

It was a mighty miracle that blessed an unexceptional young woman who did not feel worthy.

When someone asks you to pray for them, it's not just a cliché request. Many times, it is a powerful, cost-free way that you can bless them. No matter the distance, no matter the relationship, no matter the hour, no matter the day, pray. It is even more of a blessing when you pray for people that haven't asked you to pray for them.

The best part is you don't need to know how to pray. Sometimes I pray as if I'm writing a letter. Sometimes I just talk out loud and hope He hears me. Sometimes it's a song that you sing when somewhere in the middle you catch your breath and tremble as you try to get the lyrics out because you mean every word so deep inside yourself that you can't explain it to anyone else. No matter how you do it or what you do, it's not wrong. He knows your heart.

What if I told you, He hears every word? Every. Single. Time.

I know a boy. He is living proof.

Chapter 3: The Struggle is Real

*"When every day's just another struggle
And every choice is an act of war
Gotta pray
gotta press on
To the prize worth fighting for."*
*-- From the song: "Prize Worth Fighting For" by Jamie
Kimmett*

*E*very choice is an act of war.

Think about that for a moment.

Every decision you make is an opportunity. You have the choice to be angry, sad, happy. You have the chance to decide on an evil reaction or a loving reaction. You have the choice to do something right or something wrong. You have the opportunity to make your parents proud or disappoint them. You have the option to fill your kids with courage and hope or tear them down and make them believe they are worthless. You get to choose what will define you.

If you can, imagine for a moment that there is a constant war going on. Every. Day. As in every war, there are two sides. Those sides are evil and good, worry and joy, wrong and right. The one who wins the battle gets to count you on the side of their cause. The winner claims your spirit as their prize; this is a war for souls. Each team is winning souls.

Struggle is real. All of us struggle. Many times, people say, "If God is real, why do so many people struggle?" My answer: because each of you (each one of us) is that important.

Every day the Devil brings his "A" game. He can ruin a happy day with a quickness. His side wins if you are anxious, worried, do horrible things to others, or find a way to be evil. He has crafted his strategy, and he will throw you a speed bump that will disable your wagon. It slows and (sometimes to his joy) disables your travel to the other side, the right side, the team with joy. He is so cunning that he can delay you to such a degree that you give up trying, and then, another soul is his.

Several years ago, after my second divorce, I felt very discouraged. I felt unloved and unworthy. I was self-loathing. I was hurt, angry, sad, and anxious. I was at the bottom, and I couldn't seem to find my way out of the pit I'd put myself in.

Sadly, I was in a relationship with my current husband. He was right there. He had never failed me. Yet I thought he didn't like me, let alone love me. Although people surrounded me, I felt that I was desperately alone.

I crawled into bed one night, asking myself why; why am I always struggling?

That night I prayed for the Lord to remove my struggle and to give me the strength I needed to fight the depression and worthlessness I was feeling. I needed to believe I was who He said I was.

Throughout that night, I had a dream. It was as if I had an angel on one shoulder and a devil on the other. Although I couldn't see them, I could hear them.

I could hear the frightening evil voice of whom I will refer to as the Devil. He laughed at me. He said I wasn't good enough for the Angel. He said it was too late. He said I'd already given up, and getting my soul was easy. As he spoke, flashes of reddish-black flew across my eyes, as if sparks of fire when he spoke.

The Angel fought back. The Angel said I was loved, and that I brought light into the dark. The Angel demanded the Devil to leave me, and a bright white light filled my vision. Every time the Angel pushed the Devil off my shoulder, I could inexplicably feel it more than I could hear it.

I didn't wake up from that dream feeling any differently. It was just a dream. Honestly, I woke up thinking I was a whack job because of my dream. I woke up thinking the Devil was right.

I woke up and mumbled under my breath, "What difference does any of this make? Even though people are around me, and they (referring to my kids and boyfriend) are here, I am still all alone!"

I sat up in bed and angrily threw my legs over the edge of the bed to get up, but the moment my feet touched the floor, my whole world changed.

It's difficult to explain what happened, and if you don't believe me, I won't blame you.

The moment my feet touched the floor, I heard a thundering voice!

It was everywhere! It shook me. I was quite sure it was shaking the house, my room, the windows. I initially believed it was an earthquake, but someone had shouted! It shocked me so much that I fell to my knees as the words were spoken, and I bowed down until my head touched the floor.

This earth-shaking voice thundered in an authoritative way which left me fearful, but confident and loved all at the same time.

"You are NEVER alone! I AM always with you!" the voice boomed.

I have no idea how long I was there, kneeling by the side of my bed. Time seemed to stop. When I finally sat back on my heels, tears were streaming down my face. I purposefully tried to catch my breath. I looked around my room, disoriented and bewildered.

Did anyone else hear that? I thought silently. Yet no one had been stirred from their sleep. Additionally, no windows had been broken, no dishes cracked. There was no swift-moving storm, and no trees were swaying in the wind. It was then that I realized that I alone had experienced that powerful moment.

What I had heard was something inside of me, something that wasn't audible to anyone else. I knew then it wasn't meant for everyone, only for me. At that moment, I began to understand all the sermons I'd heard telling me that the same Spirit that raised Christ from the tomb was alive and well inside of me.

There is a song with lyrics that ring out "My God's not dead He's surely alive! He's living on the inside, roaring like a lion! " I wonder if the writer has experienced this same type of event. The voice I heard was a roar at a minimum. From then on, my eyes opened, and my life began to change in dramatic and positive ways. The fight from my dream wasn't a silly figment of my imagination. It was real. And better yet, my God won! I knew from that moment on that I would genuinely never again be alone.

With new understanding, I no longer lived in fear of being alone. As a result, my relationship with my partner became infinitely better. Within 12 months of that event, we would be married. Better still, I knew he loved me and that he wanted to share his life with me as much as I wanted to share mine with him.

I no longer had a fear of struggling financially, and my finances became better. I started giving more. I began to understand money to be a tool. I started to use it as a blessing, and as a result of that mindset, I got more.

When I realized that the lies you believe about yourself are the only things keeping you from living, everything I am changed.

Every day, I choose joy.

I choose.

I still have to search for it sometimes. It doesn't mean there isn't a struggle. I still have pain, sadness, and things still make me angry. Even then, joy is not something for which I wait. I choose for it to rule over the pain and the struggle.

I choose joy to be what I am.

I have joy, and I'm able to choose joy because I first have hope. Without hope, no one can find joy.

I have hope because I have faith. Faith is a word I use only to explain to others what I have that they may not have found yet. Faith is knowing you are not alone. There is more than just this.

You are more important than you could ever imagine.

Only when you realize just how important your choices are will you be able to see your struggles as merely the tireless efforts of an evil spirit trying to overpower you. So, you decide. You can choose to be light, or you can be darkness.

As for me, I'm going to shine!

Chapter 4: Wave after Wave

"For I know the plans I have for you," declares the Lord,
"plans to prosper you and not to harm you,
plans to give you hope and a future."
Jeremiah 29:11 New International Version (NIV)

The beautiful baby who struggled to breathe on his own soon became a boy, and in the blink of an eye, had grown into a young man with passion and talent for music.

He started playing the drums at two years of age. Because he was so young, no one would entertain our requests for formal lessons until he was 4. When our son was 8, his drum teacher told us that there was nothing left to teach him and encouraged us to introduce him to improvisation and playing on a stage. Shortly after, I became the mom chaperoning her child, who played in the band at the bar. Imagine! An eight-year-old!

By the time he reached high school, it seemed only natural for him to drum with drumline and marching band. His senior year, he became the lead snare drummer and led the percussion. As it would turn out, he was a natural leader. Because of his strong nature and kind heart, my son made friends with many people, some of whom were more troubled than others. His light attracted so many.

One evening, my son came to me and confessed that a freshman girl from band was keeping him up at night. It was affecting his ability to do well in school because she would start conversations late at night via social media chat.

At first, I had figured she had a crush on him, but he quickly explained that wasn't the case. He told me that this girl was somewhat of a "hidden" girl; she didn't have many friends. As he spoke, he said to me that recently she'd been talking crazy, almost scary. She'd threatened to take a bottle of pills due to depression. My son feared for her safety and that her threats would somehow become a reality if he stopped talking with her.

The disruption and threats continued for several nights. One evening during an online chat conversation, the girl started talking about the voices she was hearing. Her responses became scattered and challenging to keep up with for my son. Soon, she stopped chatting with him altogether.

After several unsuccessful attempts to reach her via chat, text, and calling, my son, very bravely and without guidance, decided to drive over to her family's house. It was 1:00 a.m. When he arrived, he hurriedly parked and ran to their front door. He pounded on the door to alert the family inside.

At first, no one came, and he became nervous they'd not heard him. He pounded again, hoping to wake the family. Just then, he heard a loud thud against the outer wall of the house near the entry. He assumed it was a door being slammed inside in frustration due to his late-night knocking.

Soon the door opened and revealed the girl's parents. My son relayed to them his concerns that their daughter may not be well. Sounding a bit troubled and vowing to check on her daughter, the mother thanked my son.

My son made his way to his car, and as he opened the car door, he heard a howling sound, much like the sound a dog would make if he were injured. Curious but tired, he got in his car and drove back home. As he got out of his car to head inside, he heard sirens. He prayed that it wasn't for his young friend.

The next morning, he awoke to a phone call. The young girl's mother had called to say that her daughter had tried to end her life. It was the prompting by my son late the previous night that alerted them to check on her. She explained that they had gone into her room and found her hanging from the ceiling fan. The mother gave her daughter CPR until the paramedics arrived. The mother said that although she was alive, she was in a coma, and her prognosis was undetermined. Through her sadness, she requested my son to come to the hospital as soon as possible.

Reluctantly, my son and I headed to the hospital. Upon his arrival, everyone hailed my boy as a hero. Graciously, he accepted their compliments, although he felt awkward taking them when this young woman confided in him, and he hadn't been able to help her more or prevent this altogether.

Her mother told my son a different story. She said to him that had he not woken them that night, they wouldn't have these moments with their daughter now, however brief they may be. She explained that she'd gotten into her daughter's room while her daughter was still swinging. It appeared she'd jumped off a chair towards the exterior wall of her room. The poor mother said that she had wailed loudly when she found her because even though my son had alerted them to possible trouble, she hadn't been expecting that.

The doctors had told the family the child could still hear but was showing few other signs of life. She was in a coma. Because of the trauma, her muscles, trachea, and vocal cords were damaged and that if they could stabilize her, she would require surgery to rebuild it all. They were uncertain how the lack of oxygen would affect her long term. So, they were taking it day by day, minute by minute.

In what could have been this child's final hours, this mother wanted my son to have a moment with her daughter, as she thought her daughter would like that. Per the child's iPad chat history, my son had been her only confidant.

Through tears, the mother thanked my son for caring enough to come in the middle of the night and to be a true friend.

With heartbroken reluctance, we entered the young lady's ICU room. She was intubated and full of monitoring wires and tubes. Many aunts, uncles, cousins, and family all patted my son on the shoulder and thanked him as they were being ushered out of the room to allow my son time alone with his friend.

My son asked me, "Mom, what do I say?"

I told him to tell her his story; that he'd died and came back.

Then I kissed her hand and told her she wasn't yet done here. I told her how my son had died too, but he'd chosen to come back, and now he'd met her.

"You must be one of the reasons he is still here," I told her. "You are so important. Maybe he was born just for this; to save you, and to help others. Everyone is waiting to love you. It's time for you to wake up now and get started living again. This is only your beginning."

Then I left her alone with my son.

Later, as we left the hospital, we called my father and told him about this incident. He said that he would pray for her. From that day on, my father would ask about her. He was quite proud of the difference his grandson had made in this young girl's life and believed that he was here for a bigger purpose; that this event was only the beginning.

Three days later, that young lady woke up. Within five days, she was out of ICU. In less than two weeks, they had transferred her to a children's hospital and she was starting to whisper. Six months later, she returned to school. Nearly a year after the incident, that young lady wrote my son a thank you note.

She thanked him for saving her life. She apologized for putting him through that and said that because of this second chance she'd gotten, she'd realized she wasn't finished here yet.

Her family and the doctors said her recovery was nothing short of a miracle.
I'd say that's about right.

What if you are someone's miracle?

What if you are raising someone else's miracle?

How many lives change because of the choices or the outcomes of life's events? Is there more going on in the bigger picture? Does everything happen for a reason?

It's like the ocean; can you count the waves in the ripple?

Chapter 5: You'll want to come to church

"Whoever believes and is baptized will be saved,
but whoever does not believe will be condemned."
Mark 16:16 New International Version (NIV)

$\mathcal{A}$s a teen, we had moved from rural Nebraska to Arizona, and despite our best efforts, we couldn't find the right church where we felt at home. My parents had tried the churches of the same denomination as those we'd attended at home, but the atmosphere was not what they wanted. Church in Arizona seemed to be for show, not for the right reasons. I didn't push to go to church. My brother and I were older, and our other family that lived nearby weren't regular church attenders. For that reason, I'm sure it seemed less urgent to get back into a church family after our move.

As I grew older, I missed having a church family. After the miraculous birth of my son, I started to seek out a church. I found a local, non-denominational church to attend and enjoyed the pastor's messages very much. I invited my parents to visit, and they started to participate with my family. I was baptized by immersion at that church in the presence of my two-year-old son and my loving parents.

My father loved the pastor, too. He felt his sermons were relatable, and the work the church was doing in the community, and globally, felt aligned with what he believed was important. However, as the years went by and the church grew, it felt less and less like the original church we'd come to know and love. The music became louder, the sermons became less personable and more big-screen-movie type and quickly, it lost its appeal to the small-town variety family like mine. Soon we were no longer attending, and the absence of church became the new normal.

Years passed by, and I moved farther and farther away from church until one day, I found myself on the floor with my head bowed down in awe and wonder. That became a realization that the church was calling again.

I spoke with my would-be-husband, and he agreed that our focus should be on finding a small church, one in which the Pastor did his job out of love for Christ rather than for church status or recognition. Thus, began our church hopping experience!

Don't be shy! Some of you know exactly what I'm talking about. Sunday comes, and you jump around from church to church, trying on the message as if it's a well-loved pair of jeans. If something about it doesn't fit, then you move on. Maybe it's the people, the building, the pastor, the coffee, who knows what! You don't commit, and it doesn't speak to you, so you just move on. That's all fine and dandy, unless you have kids.

Kids can make or break a church experience. We were guided by our children's need for the Lord more than our own. They had questions. Some of them even had their own "experiences," and they needed to find a place to share those with others beyond Grandpa, Dad, or Mom. That led us to search for the right mix of small size with a significant youth program.

Soon, we found a small neighborhood church based on Craig Groeschel's principals from Life.Church. It was a small congregation. Each Sunday, they would set up a church service inside a small storefront location that was complete with a stage for the music, lights, sound system, and seating. A second church within the building would share the responsibilities of the children's programs, which were terrific. At the end of the service, the congregation would work together to dismantle the service.

The pastor was a former accountant who felt called to ministry. Because he was a wonderfully engaging man that spoke from his heart, we enjoyed his sermons so much that we soon invited my parents. When they began attending, they agreed that this was a special place to worship.

My father was always drawn to the needy, especially those where children at need came into play. Many times, he attended to people that were not all they portrayed themselves to be. As a result, people often took advantage of his good nature.

On one occasion, my father saw a young family standing outside a grocery store begging for money. The woman had two children and a grandchild. The youngest was in a diaper and wrapped in a blanket despite the chilly fall weather. He took the family to buy them food, clothes, and a hotel room for a warm night's sleep. It was when the police were needed to make them leave the hotel room that my father discovered that the family had done this many times before and rented an apartment a short distance from the hotel.

On another occasion, my father gave a man a ride home from a park where he was fishing. The man lived in the city, far from my father's comfort zone. Being a man of his word, he decided to take the man home as he'd said he would. When they arrived at the house, the passenger stated he couldn't go in and asked to get a ride somewhere else. After doing this a few times, my father said he could no longer continue to take him around town. At that point, the man abducted my father and took over the wheel of the car. He drove aimlessly through the city all night. When he stopped at a local convenience store for more alcohol, my father was able to escape and drove to a police station.

With a history of experiences such as this, it was amazing my father had any faith at all. Broken-hearted, he spoke to the pastor about his lack of confidence in humanity and his calling to serve.

The pastor encouraged my father to become involved in works through the church as opposed to trying to help individuals on his own. Soon, with a partnership through the church, my father was teaching kids to read and working in "God's Garden" at a local children's home. He loved it!

Finding an outlet for his need to give and minister, my father was indeed in his element. Although he was hurting physically from years of abuse to both his back and knees, he was inexplicably happy. My parents continued to go to this little church even after my attendance waned.

One week my father called and asked if we were going to go to church on Sunday, to which I replied that I didn't know. We'd not been in attendance for a few weeks, and, while we did need to return, the stress of work and kids left us more apt to stay home on Sunday than to head out for church. My father countered and said that he thought we'd want to come to church this weekend. Sensing my father's urgency, I accepted his invitation and promised him we'd be there.

When we arrived that Sunday, I immediately became aware of the reason my father wanted us to join him. That Sunday, my father, just one month past his 74th birthday, decided to acknowledge his faith in Christ publicly. That Sunday, my father, with his aching knees and sore back, waded into a horse tank at the front of a little strip-mall church and was baptized!

I had always assumed that because of my father's enormous faith in God, he'd been baptized years before I was born. Little did I know that he'd never decided to go public with his belief.

That day he became even more perfect. I was so proud of his decision to be made new, and I believe he was as well.

From that day forward, my father started to live his life much more intentionally. He became a Sunday School teacher in the children's ministry at the church, where he shared with them his passion for the love of God. He even bought them Bibles as gifts at Easter. He continued his work at the children's home in the garden and teaching in Sunday School until his heart and health said otherwise.

Isn't it ironic how things always seem to happen in just the right order? Maybe you don't see it right away, but if you look back on things, there is a greater, more significant plan at work.

Each of us is a work in progress, no matter our age. Perfection is elusive and not attainable in this life. Tragedy strikes when we stop trying to be the best version of ourselves.

Chapter 6: Internal Surgery

"For you created my inmost being;
you knit me together in my mother's womb."
Psalm 139:13 New International Version (NIV)

$\mathcal{I}$ wish I could recall the exact events that led to the diagnosis, but my mind has a funny way of releasing the painful and frightening events in my life.

I only recall that my dad was rushed into the hospital due to heart trouble for which they were going to do quadruple bypass surgery. Talk about a 'moment of prayer'!

I don't know that I'd ever seen my mother so worried. Quadruple bypass in my father's medical condition seemed like a death sentence. He'd always had a struggle with his heart.

In the end, his surgery was a double bypass, which was a blessing. However, when the dust had settled on the outcome of the operation, there was a word that fell heavy at our feet.

A word we got to take home and discuss.

A word that I wish we could erase from this planet.

Cancer.

They had found tumors in my father's lungs, and they'd diagnosed him with lung cancer. Just a few weeks later, we were sitting at a desk exploring treatment options with a doctor at M.D. Anderson Cancer Center. My father was not one to enjoy going to the doctor. He had already spent enough time trying to fix numerous other health problems. His distaste wasn't going to change at this appointment.

We returned home that day with no appointment to go back—no plan of attack. No follow up. My father believed that it had been there for a long while but not presenting any problem; he wasn't going to believe that he needed some kind of chemo or radiation to fix it. He decided to live with cancer.

I was proud of him for that. Whether it was brave or stupid, I wasn't sure, but I was nevertheless pleased that he'd remained true to himself.

For Dad, living with cancer meant some lifestyle changes; more salads, less ice cream, more juices, more essential oils (okay that may have been my idea), more reading, more learning.

For the rest of us, it meant more praying and trying to keep up with what he wanted to try next.

One day I could feel his anxiousness. He'd been studying the Gerson Cancer Treatment Theory, and he wanted to try it. It was an intensive juicing diet that would require six weeks of non-stop juicing. He would need to drink a different juice every few hours, and all had to be made fresh. Additionally, he would have to stop his other medications, and he wasn't sure that would be good for his heart. He was beating himself up, trying to decide what to do.

His anxiety made him feel completely overwhelmed, and as his daughter, I was exceptionally moved by his emotional response to what he was feeling. It wasn't like my steady, strong Daddy to be struggling.

In desperation, I wrote a mindless email to a God-fearing woman with an extraordinary blog that was very upbeat. I didn't know her; I'd just been reading her blog on social media. Yet, I poured my tears into a random email and explained my father's circumstances, and what he was going through, and I shared my sadness for my father's condition, and his anxiety. I asked her to say a prayer for my father, a prayer that he may find peace in his decision.

That email was a purge. It was one of those 'I-have-nobody-to-talk-to,' late-night, rambling kind of emails and closely resembled the fabled letter to Santa. I didn't expect anyone even to read it. I just mindlessly sent it.

The next morning, I woke to her response. Not only did she read my email, but she'd personally invited me to call her.

When I called her later that day, she answered! A complete and total stranger that I'd never met cared enough to answer my call because I'd asked her to pray for my Daddy.

She explained that she was heading to yoga and would meditate on what to do, and then she would get back to me. Praying was what she knew we needed to do.

Later that evening, she wrote me an email--a prayer. She asked me to set an alarm, as would she, and every hour of the following day, we would pray the prayer she had written. Her prayer was simple yet sophisticated. She asked the Lord to fill my father with the Holy Spirit. For the Spirit to go work on my father. We prayed that every cell would break open, for the cancerous parts of the cells to disappear, and be replaced with clean, noncancerous cells. It was very detailed, and I could tell this beautiful soul took her time to get it right.

Together we prayed—all day.

The following day my father came to my home to watch a movie with my family. As he sat on the couch, he yawned sleepily, and I feared he might not make it through the film.

"Dad, you okay?" I asked. "You seem awfully tired!"

"Well," my father stated, "I don't know what's going on, really."

"What do you mean? You feel okay?" I asked him.

"Well, yes. I'm just tired. I don't know what was going on last night, but when I went to sleep, it felt like something was…"

My father shuffled his hands like a child in his lap, kind of making a knitting motion. "Something was, well it kinda felt like something, or someone," to which he gave me a look I'd come to learn meant 'pay attention,' "was doing surgery inside me. You know, I'm not really sure, but I don't think I have cancer anymore. I kind of feel like I don't."

"Really?" I said. "Well. Isn't that somethin'!"

At my father's next Doctor visit, nearly three months later, they did several scans and determined that the large tumors had all but stopped growing while the smaller tumors were almost gone. At that time, his Doctor gave him the green light to keep doing what he was doing as it was working.

That day I wrote an email again to the beautiful soul with the blog, and I told her about the doctor visit. We both silently celebrated our prayerful victory.

I never told my Dad about the prayer.

Scan after scan, my father never reported a change in his tumors. He seemed to carry on as if the cancer was never diagnosed and never really changed anything. He lived with lung cancer for quite a while after that.

He went on to teach Sunday School, build upright planter gardens with his Grandson and laugh, take goofy pictures, and spoil all of us with his presence.

The only ones who have ever known about that prayer are me, God, and a woman I've never seen.

Sometimes, only God can do the surgery you need.

Sometimes, He is the only one who can mend that which is broken.

Chapter 7: The Line

"Why, you do not even know what will happen tomorrow.
What is your life?
You are a mist that appears for a little while
and then vanishes."
John 4: 14 New International Version (NIV)

In May of 2018, a man traveling home from work on a local freeway witnessed an accident just in front of him. A car in front of him, going more than sixty miles per hour, suddenly veered into a wall and crashed head-on. The man, who was on the phone with his wife, stated he was going to stop and help the injured person. He said he'd call her right back and hung up.

Hours went by, and she never received a call back. Something inside her filled her with dread. She began checking in with other family members to see if they'd heard from her husband. Then, she listened to the news.

A local news station was reporting about a good Samaritan that was run over on the freeway trying to help an injured person in an accident. Although too soon to identify the victim, the news reported that the man was taken to a local hospital with serious, life-threatening injuries. The woman could feel that something terrible was coming.

Soon after, the call came. The woman learned her husband had indeed been the good samaritan; his injuries were too significant to overcome. He had been taken too soon; their family forever changed.

This man was my father's best friend; a friend he'd been fishing with and watched become a father. A person that my father had helped become the helpful and selfless man he was until his last day. A friend that my father would never want to lose. I was going to have to share the unfortunate news, and it would be so much more difficult given my father's fragile state.

A few months before the accident, my father's health had begun to decline rapidly. Several times since then, he'd had instances of falling without the ability to get back up. He'd stopped sleeping in his bed and instead moved to a recliner in the living room. His ability to care for himself was slowly slipping away. As a result, my brother and I were taking turns being with him when my mother had commitments outside the home. Over the course of just a few short weeks, my father was sleeping more and more. He also began telling big-fish kind of stories; the kind that didn't make a lot of sense and worried us.

As the news of his friend's passing spread through the regular channels, I was unsure what to do. My mother, overwhelmed with the responsibility of caring for my dad, was starting to look increasingly exhausted, and her emotions ran high. I didn't want to cause her or my father any further unrest. Because my father liked to stay connected with his friends via Facebook and watched their profiles closely, I knew he would see it eventually. Not only would it be on Facebook, but because the accident was local, it had already been broadcast on the news and would likely be reshown. If the news reached my father through television or social media, I feared it would intensify the symptoms of his illness. Therefore, my mother and I decided it would be best to gently let him know.

Let there be no misunderstanding; there is no way to gently tell someone their best friend was killed in a freeway accident. When we told him, my father was sitting at the kitchen table in his favorite chair; the spot he would sit and watch the world go by from the dining room window. I crouched down and gently put my hands on my father's knees. I asked him if he'd seen the news about the freeway accident with the man who was a good samaritan. He replied he had. I then explained it was his friend.

With care, concern, and disbelief, my father looked me in the eyes, trying to understand.

"It was?" he asked.

"Yes, Daddy," I replied.

"Is he okay?" my father asked.

"No, Dad, he isn't. He didn't make it, Dad. I'm sorry. Do you understand, Dad? He died from his injuries. He's gone." I got on my knees in front of him so that our eyes met, and he could see my pain.

It was only then that I could see understanding in my father's eyes. As anguish washed across his face, my father began to sob in massive waves. We all surrounded him and laid our hands on him, offering our support.

"Oh, Lord! Are there no good days left?" he shouted out to God with a broken heart.

A few weeks later, we attended the memorial service. My father cried through the service and seemed lost in thought. He was full of regret over what he perceived as unresolved conflicts; words left unspoken. There had been no time to say goodbye. There was no opportunity to tell his friend how much he'd genuinely cared for him.

As the weeks went by, life began to return to what it had been. My father was still sleeping in the recliner and struggling to stay awake most of the time. Often my mother would catch him wildly spinning his hands in a circle while he was sleeping.

We discussed my father's actions with his hands and talked about what he may be doing in his sleep. Perhaps he was fishing and reeling in his line? Maybe he was sowing seeds? He did love to garden. None of us knew for sure.

Soon, my mother noticed him making the actions while he was awake. She knew he was watching television with her, but at random times throughout the day, he would suddenly reach out and appear to try to catch something. He would then reel it in and stuff something into his clasped hand.

One day, while my father and I were alone together, I asked him about the movements he had been doing with his hands. I asked him if he was fishing with his friend. He stated he had been fishing many times with him in his dreams, but that wasn't what he was doing. He then went on to explain his actions.

"When your Uncle was in the hospital, and I would set with him, there were several times when he would act as if he was trying to catch something. He would even ask me if I saw 'the line,' and he'd ask me to capture it for him. After several days of this, I decided he really could see something I couldn't. So, the next time he asked me to catch it, I would try. If he said I caught it, I would then stuff it into his hand so he could hang onto it."

"What was it?" I asked.

"I didn't know then what it was, but I do now," my father explained. "You can't see it, can you?" he asked.

"No, I can't. Maybe I don't know what I'm looking for." I responded, intrigued.

"It's a line... a wispy thread. It almost looks like a mist as it moves by me, but it's not. It's a line. Like a fishin' line," Dad continued.

As always, I was listening intently to what my father said. I gently apologized for not being able to see what he saw. Then I asked him, "Where does the line start? And where does it end?"

Lovingly and excitedly, my father pointed to his heart and said, "Well, it starts right here. Then it goes like this..." He moved his finger up and down in a zig-zag motion moving away from his chest. "Then it just goes..." and he moved his finger in a straight line away from him toward the ceiling.

I giggled and asked, "Where is....?" as I made the same motion he had, following the line he'd drawn.

My dad quickly pointed repeatedly at the ceiling with a mischievous grin. "I don't know. Up there, I guess! That's why I keep trying to hold onto that line. If I can catch it, I can hold on just a little bit longer."

Days later, I realized the imaginary line my father had drawn that day was an EKG line from a heart monitor. The first zig-zag line was depicting the beating of a heart. The flat line represented the end of a life and the stopping of a heart. The ascension of the line meant the release of a spirit to heaven.

I believe the mist my father spoke of was his life. The line he reached for would provide him the ability to choose when it was time to give up his spirit. Thus, he reached for it and tried to hang on. On that day, at that time, he was not yet done here.

My father was trying to hang on, if only for just a while longer.

Our days are numbered and fleeting, like sands through an hourglass. When your heart line becomes a flat line, where will it end?

Chapter 8: Broken

"24 How many are your works, LORD! In wisdom you
made them all; the earth is full of your creatures.
25 There is the sea, vast and spacious,
teeming with creatures beyond number—
living things both large and small."
Psalm 104: 24-25 New International Version (NIV)

My husband grew up in and around Anchorage.
Ironically, my father had been assigned to Fort Richardson,
Alaska, when he served in the Army. Between the two of
them, I heard all about the beauty and majesty of the state.

My father described Alaska as unexplainably beautiful; nothing else like it in the whole world. Often, he talked about the yearning to, once again, experience the endless rivers and tall mountain peaks cropping up out of the blue waters of the ocean. He had once taken my mother on an executive retreat Alaskan cruise, courtesy of his employer.

My husband talked of forests, endless trails, the cold, and mountains. He would tell strangers, "Many people only dream of going to Alaska in their lifetime. My recommendation is if you ever get the chance to go, GO! Don't wait, or you'll never make it." He still says that to this very day.

So, when given a chance, that's exactly what we did.

One September day, my husband's uncle called to let us know he was coming into Phoenix. We offered him a place to stay for the weekend. While he was with us, he mentioned an upcoming family reunion in Anchorage scheduled for July 2018. On a whim, I checked the price of flights from Phoenix to Anchorage, and they were unbelievably low.

Because the cost of taking my family of 6 to Alaska had been prohibitive, we'd never gone. However, I'd found rates showing a total of only $1800 for all of us to fly to Alaska. That seemed exceptionally reasonable.

Thankfully, my husband had just finalized the details of becoming the owner of a well-established business and was sure that he could work out a vacation. So, with my eyes closed and my fingers crossed, I purchased six round-trip tickets for an unforgettable vacation to beautiful Alaska.

We ordered every free brochure about Alaska we could get and began the process of deciding what things our children would see. We started counting down to our departure on July 1st. Each day that we crossed off on our calendar brought more anticipation. We planned to do many things on our trip. We arranged for a visit to a wildlife preserve, a hike on a glacier, ice skating, and zip-lining. We also planned stays in Denali Park (where we would see Mount McKinley on a crystal-clear day with no clouds), another in a tiny town called Talkeetna, and a cabin on the Kenai River with fishing and a river float. We were ready to make memories together.

My father was so excited for us. He couldn't wait for his grandchildren to experience the beauty of Alaska. A large part of him wanted to join us, and if there would've been a way, I would've done anything to take him with us. Unfortunately, my father's health had been significantly deteriorating that summer.

For a few months leading up to our vacation, my father started having a difficult time getting up from his sleeping spot or a chair. Often his legs would swell, and his blood sugar levels would cause him to be confused. Occasionally he could not answer simple questions with clear answers. Although it was difficult, my mother silently carried the weight of caring for my father all by herself. They were both suffering.

The reality of it was my father was dying. He had told me once that he was ready to go "home." For months leading up to our family vacation, I'd been watching him prepare for his final trip.

I was beginning to question whether I should go to Alaska at all. If he became severely ill, I would want to be with him. If my father were to pass away while we were there, we would all need to come home. My father picked up on the worry I was carrying, and he called me one day.

"Don't worry," he'd said. "I will call you every day while you are away. It will be just like you are here."

He continued to tell me how important it was for me to take the trip and have fun with my family; that he wouldn't want us to miss it for the world. He told me my husband and I had worked so hard, and that we deserved this once in a lifetime trip.

We had worked very hard and were looking forward to this rare opportunity to travel as a family. With his words of encouragement pounding in my heart, I decided we would go.

Meanwhile, I choked back my tears of fear. I wrote a letter to my father with strict instructions that it would be given to him only if it was evident I wouldn't make it back for his final moment. My oldest, who had stayed behind, knew that he was to read it to my father only in the case of an emergency.

Then, pushing my feelings of unease aside, and trying to be the wild mom my kids loved me to be, we set out for Alaska.

I planned two ways to help my father hold on for our return.

When I was in high school, I'd decided to leave home for a summer and travel to stay with a friend's family in Utah. It was a 6-hour drive. At not quite seventeen, alone and without GPS, my father gave his blessing, and I left on my adventure. I had no idea that I would miss my family so much. My father would write me letters nearly every day. Maybe he missed me too, but I believe he was just keeping me positive. It worked.

My Alaska trip was the perfect opportunity to respond in kind. I decided we would each buy him a postcard wherever we stopped, and we'd mail them back home to him. That way he could enjoy our trip with us.

I also called upon his friends and family from Nebraska and Colorado to come visit him. Two groups of his family would make the journey to be with him at different times, but their trips would overlap by one glorious weekend.

We scheduled the visits for the first two weeks of July. They laughed, told old stories, played music, and ate well. They were the most important events I've ever planned. We didn't know it at the time, but it was the last time my father would see his sister, sisters-in-law, niece, nephew, and many friends who were like family.

I called my parents daily to share our experiences. Each day, my father would talk less and less on the phone until finally, my mother was doing all the talking. Looking back, I realize that was God's way of breaking the habit I had of talking to my father. He was my greatest confidant and my biggest fan. Keeping our conversations short, and not speaking to dad, allowed me to focus on the kids and their experience. It also prepared me for a future where my father wouldn't be there to talk to.

Alaska was great! We did it all, literally. There wasn't anything my kids didn't get to experience. We fished, hiked on a glacier, saw wildlife, and Mount McKinley, and we also saw the rehabilitated areas from my father's pictures of downtown Anchorage from the 1964 earthquake. We made memories that my family will never forget. It was the trip of a lifetime that most people only dream of taking. We put over 2500 miles on a rental car traveling up and down Alaska's coast, and we hiked over 30 miles during that trip.

We spent our final week winding down in a cabin on the Kenai Peninsula. It was a quaint two-bedroom, rustic cottage with modern amenities. Just off the front porch was a section of woods overlooking the river from a bluff, and behind the cabin was an abandoned, broken greenhouse.

Sadly, without the excitement of extended family around to raise his spirits, my father's health declined even more. During a doctor's appointment, the medical staff advised my mother to take him to the hospital for admission. Although my mother hadn't wanted to call and worry me, I found out the day we checked into our cabin.

Worry, I did. I tried to hide it but was secretly sick about it. When sadness and fear would occasionally take over, I would go outside with my camera and start taking pictures. Many times, very early in the morning, and sometimes in the middle of the night, I would find myself outside trying to capture the beauty of the broken greenhouse in the midnight sun.

The dilapidated greenhouse was strikingly beautiful in the sunsets and sunrises. It became my favorite subject to photograph. The exterior of the little building was a weathered white patina, with years of dust settled on the panes of glass in the ceiling and door. Rays of light would separate in the dust, making an almost mystical haze inside. Inside, the pots and tools were strewn about on their sides, as if someone had quickly discarded them. Oddly, I felt connected to my father every time I was near that greenhouse. He'd loved to garden until he'd become ill. This little crumbling building, though falling apart and weathered, was full of light, just like my father.

Light would pour through the greenhouse and illuminate the inside. It seemed as if I could open the door and let it spill out, but I wasn't allowed to touch it. The owner of the property was adamant about not going inside, let alone opening the doors of the greenhouse. I understood as it was likely because of the structural fragility and risk of injury. It was similar to being unable to help, or be with, my father. Anytime the sadness would take over, I would sneak away, camera in hand, with a hope to capture the light inside the greenhouse. Most times, it was impossible.

In the early morning hours of our second to last day in the cabin, my cell phone rang out "Daddy's Girl,"; the song I had chosen as a ringtone for my father. I was startled awake. It was early, and I hadn't expected my phone to ring from the ledge of the window. The ringing was remarkable because our cabin had such spotty cellular service that there were only two spots that had reception. Unless you were standing perfectly still in one of those specific spaces, no cell phone would work.

Knowing it was him, I answered, "Hey, Dad, what's up?"

"Well, where are you?" he asked. I said I was still in Alaska. He apologized, saying he'd forgotten. When he asked how much longer I would be there, I explained that I had only a couple more days, and then we'd be home.

"For some reason, I thought you were already home," he stated.

I told him that he'd know when I was home because I would be right there with him.

"That's good because then there will be no more problems," he said.

"Problems? What's going on? Are you okay? What problems?" I asked.

"Well, I am stuck in this bed on the top of a building, and I can't get off the bed to go. I can't find your mother," he stated, irritated but clear.

He sounded fearful, so I immediately reminded him he was in the hospital in a room, not on a roof, and mom had gone home to shower since it was the middle of the night. I told him he was going to have to wait just a bit longer, but I'd have someone help so he'd know he wasn't on top of a building. Then he said he knew he was in the hospital, and I should just finish my trip and get home.

That was the call that told me; my dad was ready for me to come home. I needed to get back.

I immediately called the nurses station at the hospital and asked someone to check on Dad as he had sounded fearful of being alone. I called my mother, who had showered and planned to catch some restful sleep. Exhaustedly, she said that she would head back to the hospital. Having made all the necessary calls, I hung up the phone and sat with the realization that my father was waiting for me before making the final journey home.

A few hours later, I spoke to my brother and mentioned the midnight phone call. My brother chalked it up to another episode of Dad's increasing confusion. I needed him to understand. With a lump in my throat, I explained to him my deep understanding; I knew my father was telling me it was time for him to go. I said that I expected he'd take that opportunity as soon as I returned. My brother sounded irritated by my belief.

Now, you may be wondering why I put this chapter in this book. It's no miracle.

Or is it?

Is it a miracle that my dad let me know he was waiting for me?

Is it a miracle that my dad told me he was trying to leave?

Is it a miracle when your loved one gives you an indication that they are going to be gone soon so that you can bring together all the people they loved one final time?

Is it a miracle when your loved one gives you the chance to say goodbye?

I believe in miracles.

Chapter 9: Twenty-six

"For we must all appear before the judgment seat of
Christ, so that each of us may receive what is due us for the
things done while in the body, whether good or bad."
2 Corinthians 5:10 New International Version (NIV)

We flew in on a red-eye from Anchorage to Phoenix,
where I rushed to my father's bedside. His condition hadn't
changed much, no improvement. I was so happy to be home
with him. Little did I know it would be our last few days
together.

That first day home, I relieved my Mother of her watch duties. Dad spoke so quietly that I found myself crawling into his bed to listen more carefully. I'd longed to be close to him since we'd left.

Later, my husband brought our boys up to the hospital. As they entered the room, my Dad lovingly offered hugs, kisses, and smiles. The boys told stories of our trip, sharing all their favorite parts. My father listened, participated, and smiled. Knowing their Grandpa had always been a fan of ice cream, they'd stopped and bought him a chocolate "Frosty" from a nearby Wendy's. Although his diet may have been compromised in the eyes of the hospital dietician, any day was a good day for ice cream in the eyes of his grandsons.

He took one bite and said, "Ooooohhhh, that's good!" like a small child tasting ice cream for the first time.

That day was precious and fleeting. Exhaustion eventually set in, and my family and I left to return home. My mother, renewed by a shower and a nap, took over.

After returning to the hospital the following day, my mother explained it hadn't been a good night. He'd been restless. His thoughts had become scattered, he sounded confused, and he appeared to be in pain. It was evident she needed a break, and when I arrived, I gave her a break to get in a shower and a reprieve.

While she was gone, I crawled into his hospital bed again. He snuggled me and said he was so glad I was home.

"Now, there will be no more problems," he said again. I worried about what he meant, but understood I didn't want to know.

We talked for a while, and he shared some of his insecurities about being sick. Soon, he became tired and said, "Well, I have to go now. Okay?"

I asked him where he was going, and he said, "Nowhere really, but I have to go. I'll be back." He made his funny face at me, indicating there was more to the story, but his mischievous side wasn't ready to share yet.

"Go ahead. I'll be right here," I replied.

That was the first of many times my father would "need to go," and he would drift off to sleep, and then a while later, he'd wake up. Upon waking, he'd show varied emotions, sometimes happy, sometimes sad and crying, other times bewildered and confused. Each time, before he would fall asleep, he would announce his leaving and that he would be back.

On one occasion, my father woke crying. Nervous, I asked him what was wrong and offered to get the nurse for him. He stated he didn't want the nurse, and he explained this was a pain no medicine could fix. My father began to tell how his pain was no longer of the physical kind. His pain was in "the returning" as he called it.

My father continued to explain when he was "leaving," he believed he physically left this side of the spirit world. When he had to return, he physically had to return; and he explained the returning pain. It hurt because he could see all the pain and suffering on this side, and it was worse than any pain he'd ever physically endured.

As he explained this phenomenon he was experiencing, he appeared to be manifesting this suffering as physical pain. I tried to comfort him, but as I dried his tears, he sadly repeated his goodbye. Then he seemed to drift off to sleep instantly.

I always accepted his goodbye with an "I love you" and an ounce of anxiety; I never really knew if he was going to come back. I assumed he was coming back because he always indicated that he would, but my heart wasn't so sure. I always seemed to be holding my breath until he would wake again.

On another occasion, my father woke seemingly in more pain than he'd been in before. He woefully cried, "There is suffering. Oh, Lord, the suffering. Jesus promised he would take the pain, but he cannot take the suffering. There is so much suffering!"

To comfort him, I asked, "What is it that causes the suffering so much? Can I take it away?"

His response both warmed my heart and made it ache.

He stated there was nothing I could do. He knew he would have to leave us all behind, and that hurt him because we couldn't go where he was going, not yet.

"That suffering," he stated, "is the greatest of all. Things are never going to be the same."

I knew he was right.

With each sleeping event, he became increasingly more difficult to understand. I could see him straining to make sense of his words. He was struggling to make himself clear and understandable. Being a lifelong storyteller, this was very unlike my father.

I also began to recognize that my father was counting down each time he would go to sleep. For instance, he would say, "30 more", then drift off, sometimes in pain, sometimes in sorrow, sometimes angrily. The next time as he signed off for sleep, he'd say "29 more". I'd been trying to understand his counting backward, as it seemed he really wanted me to know, and understand, what it was.

"Twenty-six more..." he stated in a less than enthusiastic manner. Most people in the room didn't know what he was talking about or how to respond.

After trying to wrap my mind around the countdown for a while, I finally asked him, "You have to go twenty-six more times?" to which he responded, "Yes, I guess so."

My heart couldn't believe my ears. Was my dad giving me a timeline? I noted the time on the wall was 11:15 a.m. I thought to myself, "If he's counting down the hours, that means he will be leaving us about 1:15 p.m. tomorrow." For the next 24 hours, I was paralyzed; I couldn't leave the hospital. Although I hadn't told my mother about the countdown, she insisted on staying as well. They rolled in a bed for my mother to rest while I sat quietly beside my father, who continued waking in various states of awareness and emotion.

At one point, my father woke restlessly, questioning his faith.

"I guess I don't understand God!"

Anxiously, he stated that he'd been asking God to help him, but there was no help from the Lord. He felt as though all his unanswered prayers meant that God had left him. He struggled to continue to believe. My father stated he didn't think there was going to be an end to the sleep episodes of always going and then returning. Exhausted, he returned to sleep. I wept for my father. I never thought I would see my steadfast father shaken in faith.

Inexplicably, I knew that each time my father claimed he "had to go" it wasn't a choice; it was a calling. There was something more than a conscious decision to sleep. When that someone or something called him, he would always apologize for leaving, and go, even for the briefest of moments. Upon waking the next time, he seemed just a little bit bewildered to be back with us. It was as if he had physically left us only to return unexpectedly again.

When my father woke the following morning, the hospitalist came to see him. The doctor, an Indian gentleman who practiced Hindu, and had a kind bedside manner, approached my father. As he had many times before, the doctor began to verify my dad's coherence by asking him a series of questions. Usually, my father would give the standard answers: his date of birth, full name, etc. This time, however, was different.

When the doctor asked, "Do you know who you are?" he looked into the doctor's eyes and said, "Yeah! Yes, I know who I am! Don't you know? My name is Jesus Christ!" He laughed a confident laugh, then looked at the doctor and stated something so profound...

With boldness, he took the doctor by the hand and said, "Don't you know! You are Jesus Christ, too!"

Confused, the doctor shook his head and left the room. It was so profound that, in that moment, I knew my father was coherent!

Throughout the morning, my father's spirits seemed to rise. He joked with everyone and asked for back rubs. He then asked my uncle to scratch his back, to which my uncle lovingly obliged. As I began to help scratch my father's back at his request, he chuckled.

"What's so funny?" I asked him.

"Violet says you are horrible back scratchers!" my father whispered between giggles. Violet was his beloved cousin who'd passed away just a few months before.

My father's doctors came to discuss his condition later that morning. They advised that the cancer that had been in his lungs had metastasized into other organs including his liver. The medical staff requested that he get an MRI as there was concern that it had spread to his brain.

Throughout the discussions, they continued to contend that the treatments remaining for his condition were minimally successful for someone in his state. It was those discussions that led us to consider alternatives for care. Dad's time at the hospital was nearing an end as there were no additional means to treat his condition successfully.

As the afternoon approached, my father asked for his family to gather around him. He also spoke of wanting his pastors to come to see him. I anxiously watched the clock while we urgently tried to reach family and his two favorite pastors. Everyone came as quickly as they could.

When the first pastor arrived, my sweet father welcomed him with thanks. Together they prayed. My father listened intently as the pastor read scripture to him. The urgency had subsided and was replaced by patience, care, and love. It was like two old friends having an agreeable conversation that meant so much to them both.

When the second pastor arrived, my father's welcome was more restless and urgent. The young, vibrant, pastor of my father's church family, sat quietly beside him. My father genuinely loved and believed in his young pastor. He'd always spoken so highly of him.

With worry in his eyes, he shared with our Pastor his fear that he'd failed the Lord. He explained his sins to his pastor, who, in turn, reminded him of faith and forgiveness. My father encouraged the Pastor to continue the marvelous work he was doing among people. He stressed the importance of the young Pastor's messages and asked him to pass on an additional message; "Obey first! Believe it; it's real. Always obey first. Don't delay. You tell them!" The Pastor comforted him and assured him he would share.

As things started to settle down, and the twenty-sixth hour of the countdown approached, my father became restless. A large gathering of family encircled him in his room. He began to talk about leaving again, but this time was different. He was agitated and seemingly frustrated with everyone hovering.

Suddenly, my father burst out, "Oh, everyone GO! Get out of here! Forgive and go. Love each other. Forever and always. Now GO, EVERYONE!" Shocked and in disbelief, we all rushed out of his room into the waiting area.

Awkwardly, we all sat together in a quiet room with hushed whispers. My uncle paced the hallway and spoke to his wife on the phone. My husband and I held hands and took deep breaths. We discussed my father's need to be alone so that he could make peace in his own time. No one knew what to do or what to say. After what seemed like an eternity, my mother looked fearfully at me as she stood up and headed back into my father's room. After a few moments, I reluctantly followed.

As I pushed open the door, I looked at my father's face. He was completely coherent as his eyes met mine. Hesitantly, I asked him if he wanted us to come back in.

With a half-smile and a roll of his eyes he said, "I guess so." It was then I realized that he was staying for us, not himself.

Everyone returned, and eventually, the minutes wound down on the twenty-sixth hour. I held my breath each time my father fell asleep, thinking it would be the last time I told him I loved him. However, with the approach of the 27th hour, his breathing didn't cease; his condition didn't dramatically worsen. Instead, he woke up and smiled.

I leaned in close to him as he tried to speak.

"Not yet," he whispered, smiling.

It was as if he'd known I'd been counting down. "No?" I asked.

"Nope. In the early morning hours," he smiled as he squeezed my hand.

Just like that, the suffering was over. My dad wasn't upset or hurting. He was happy!

Many times, we hear of people who tell of seeing their lives flash before their eyes when faced with a near-death experience. Have we taken the time to decipher what that means? Is it really just a saying?

Scripture tells us that we will all have to account for the things we did in the body, both good and bad. Could it be that people who are on the brink of death get this review of their lives so that they can be held accountable for their actions during this life?

Just as Stephen met Jesus when he was stoned in Acts chapter 7 of the Bible, I believe our Lord Jesus comes to meet us in death. At that time, there is an accounting of our time on Earth. Not that it's a time of reward or punishment (See 2 Corinthians 5:10), but rather that we will simply meet Jesus. There will be an examination of the way we lived our lives in the years we spent here, whether we spend six, twenty-six, or seventy-eight years.

In the end, the Bible says Jesus blesses the believers with far more than we can imagine here on earth. That is the great hope. We hope to find favor in the eyes of the Lord, and not to disappoint him, just as we wouldn't want to disappoint our Earthly father (or parent). To live by faith simply means to hope to find favor and be rewarded in Heaven by the One who gave us a purpose from the beginning.

My father always said, "What harm is there to live by Faith? Faith brings peace and comfort and joy. If you have no faith, there is no hope. Without hope, life would be miserable."

What will be the outcome of your life's examination? Did you live by faith? Did you lose all hope? Maybe you've done both. Will you be proud of your life? Will you have regret? Can you use your losses, and disappointments, to create lessons from which others can learn?

It's never too late to become a blessing.

Chapter 10: One-hundred-seventy-eight

"26 So do not be afraid of them, for there is nothing
concealed that will not be disclosed,or hidden that will not
be made known.
27 What I tell you in the dark, speak in the daylight; what
is whispered in your ear, proclaim from the roofs.
28 Do not be afraid of those who kill the body
but cannot kill the soul.
Rather, be afraid of the One who can destroy
both soul and body in hell.
29 Are not two sparrows sold for a penny? Yet not one of
them will fall to the ground outside your Father's care
30 And even the very hairs
of your head are all numbered."
Matthew 10: 26-30 New International Version (NIV)

$\mathcal{I}$watched my father's eyes as the twinkle had returned, and there was a look of childlike wonder in his face.

"You look like you're feeling better," I said, smiling.

He nodded and smiled and asked for a drink. I gave him a sip of water, and as he savored it, he began to smile again.

"Oh!" he exclaimed, "It's so beautiful!" he excitedly explained.

"What's beautiful, Dad?" I asked.

"Oh, I wish you could see it!" he looked deep into my eyes, and a small tear ran down his cheek on the right side of his face.

I wiped his tear, and, to not miss a word, I climbed into bed beside him and laid my head on his shoulder.

"What does it look like, Daddy?" I asked.

"It's like the biggest, most beautiful park you've ever seen! The colors! Oh! The colors! They are so bright!" he exclaimed.

Full of wonder, I asked, "Is there a river or trees? Can you describe it to me, Dad?"

"The only word I can use to describe it is... paradise!"

I told him it sounded beautiful and that I wished I could see it too. For a while, he just lay there smiling and talking peacefully. A while later, he quietly asked for my mom to hold him. She bent over him, wrapped him in a tight hug, and kissed him sweetly. He started talking about "the beautiful shores", and my mother began to sing to him. For a time, there was peace in that room.

My oldest son brought in a guitar and played praise and worship songs. My father raised his hands in worship with my son. My son's father had also come to see him, and he enjoyed watching this special moment unfold between our son and his grandpa.

It seemed everyone was enjoying their time with my dad. However, in the background, hard decisions were being made. As a family, we'd decided to take Dad out of the hospital and bring him back home. We understood the painful immunology treatments had only a 5% chance of working for those in good health. His condition compromised even the best of chances of survival. He'd already declined the MRI of his brain because he believed it wouldn't make any difference. He had also stated that if things progressed to that degree, he wouldn't opt for treatment anyway.

There was nothing more the hospital could do for him and sending him home with in-home hospice care seemed a reasonable option. As we arranged the details, my father continued to love on everyone in the room, including his nurses.

My father lay peacefully for a large part of the day. When they came to retake his blood, he was upset. The days of being a human pin cushion had taken their toll, and with the shake of my head, the nurses left.

With a sigh of relief, I moved to my father's side.

"Do you want to go home?" I'd asked him.

Enthusiastically and with tears in his eyes, he replied, "Oh yes, please!"

I explained how we'd worked to get a nurse to help Momma, and he could go home and sleep in his room tomorrow night if that's what he wanted.

Again, he confirmed he would like that very much. Then he said he needed to go to return to sleep.

As he prepared to leave us yet again, he explained that he was excited because he was going to meet "the twelve heads of the nations"!

I didn't understand what he was saying. I asked him, "There are countries where you've been going, huh?"

With a curious expression, he replied, "I guess so! Or at least I'm going to find out!"

He was so excited to find out what was waiting for him in the world we couldn't see. He closed his eyes to sleep and, for the first time in what felt like days, so did I. Knowing he was coming home made sleeping a bit easier.

Everyone seemed to busy themselves preparing for my father's return. We had to rearrange the existing bedroom to accommodate the new hospital bed, buy sheets, and much more. Additionally, my mother had asked us to join her in finalizing a burial plot purchase at the cemetery where my dad had chosen his final resting place. While everyone was working, my oldest stayed with his grandfather until I could get back to the hospital.

Upon my return to the hospital, I found my father resting peacefully. My son and I quietly shared a conversation about our excitement to take my father home. Slowly my father began to wake. He seemed to be crying, but it wasn't pain or sadness that filled his eyes.

My son and I sat on either side of my father in his hospital bed. Sweetly, my father took each of our hands in his. He opened his eyes and spoke deliberately but quietly.
"One hundred seventy-eight."

I could tell from his expression; they were tears of joy!

Not understanding, my son and I asked him to repeat what he was saying.

"One hundred seventy-eight!" he exclaimed a bit louder as he gave us a thumbs up with each of his hands and a huge smile!

"One hundred seventy-eight?" I asked. "What is one hundred seventy-eight?"

Again, my father restated, "One hundred seventy-eight!" with more enthusiasm and another thumbs up.

His contagious excitement was evident in the way he smiled. I'd seen this smile before when he was full of pride. I could tell, whatever this was, he was very proud and excited about this.

"One hundred seventy-eight what, Grandpa?" my son asked.

"That's how many!" my father explained.

"How many what?" we asked, mirroring his excitement.

"That's how many people came to know Jesus Christ because of me," he tearfully responded with pride.

The strength in his grip, and the smile on his face, were all I needed to reassure me that he believed it.

"Is that your count or God's count?" I asked.

Slowly and deliberately, my father responded, "Both!"

I cried with joy at his excitement. I hugged him and told him how wonderful that was, and I complimented him for his accomplishment.

I told him he should be so proud, to which he replied, "I am! Oh, I am!"

As if excessively tired, he fell asleep nearly immediately. For a short while, he slept quietly. My son left, and again, I was left alone with my father. I sat beside his bed, watching his breathing, wondering if he was aware that I was in the room. I prayed for him as we sat together. I prayed that his pain was over, and that peace filled him. I prayed that the things he believed were happening were real. I prayed that in the end, others he'd loved and lost would be there to meet him when he left us to sleep the very last time.

I was brought out of my prayerful trance by the sound of my father crying. He'd woken and was quietly crying. I moved closer to him and asked him what was wrong as I dried his tears. This time his face was not shining. These were tears of sadness.

"Eight," my father said, defeated.

"Eight?" I asked. "What's eight?"

"Eight people," my father said again in despair.

"What about the eight people?" I asked my father.

"That's how many people were lost, even though I tried to tell them. They wouldn't listen. Eight people I told that refused to hear. They didn't believe me," and my father wept. His heart had broken for the ones that could not be saved. He was just as distressed about those eight as he had been over the suffering the day before.

I was not surprised. It was my father's nature to be more concerned with helping others than anything else in life. Why should it be any different as the clock ticked by in his final hours?

After all, he was emulating Jesus Christ. He was love and light.

One hundred seventy-eight people believed in the light he'd called Christ that burned so brightly inside him. Those people chose to believe and to experience that grace for themselves. In his final days, that was his defining moment. Yet, he grieved the loss of eight. Those eight that he could call by name wouldn't be with him in paradise, and he mourned for them. Just as Christ does, as God does. Shouldn't we all?

Some of you may be thinking that this is all too much to believe.

Trust me; I have been in your shoes. I know it seems unbelievable. Even though I am a believer, I, too, wondered if my father was about his wits as his consciousness ebbed and flowed. The stories he told were full of wonder. For months I questioned what he saw or believed he saw.

Not being a biblical scholar, I would never have known what my father was experiencing had it not been for a sermon our family Pastor gave on heaven. This sermon convinced me that my father was seeing and experiencing real things. These are real things we just can't see yet.

In the Bible (Luke 23), is a famous scripture. It's one many of us have heard several times regarding the crucifixion of Jesus. This passage tells of the dialogue between Jesus and others being crucified alongside him. One asks Jesus not to forget him when he "comes into His Kingdom." In verse 43, Jesus states, "Truly I tell you; you will be with me in paradise." (Luke 23:43 New International Version)

Paradise!

The Greek meaning of "paradise" is literally "enclosed park." The Hebrew language defines it as "a garden." My father spoke of this most beautiful park he could only explain as "paradise." The way he spoke of it led me to believe the paradise my father saw was heaven. Heaven is real!

When our loved ones enter their final days, they often begin to speak of those who've passed before them. It's not because they're not lucid, it's because they are actually with the ones they've lost; those who are now in that place of peace, rest, and refreshment. We know this because Jesus told the others being crucified beside him that they would be together. My father was spending time with his beloved cousin, Violet, who'd said we were horrible back scratchers (see page 73). She was in paradise. Let that comfort you! Take it into your heart and let it rest there a while. Call it what you want, but I know that my father is in paradise, and I will see him there.

A bit earlier in this chapter, I told you of my father's excitement about meeting the "heads of the nations." In the book of Revelation in the bible, they speak of a river with a tree of life that bears twelve crops of fruit. In the second verse, it states, "the leaves of the tree are for the healing of the nations" (Revelation 22:2 New International Version). Isn't it ironic that my father spoke of twelve heads of nations, and here this passage refers to twelve crops of fruit that bear leaves for healing "the nations"?

As we approach the hour of our death, I believe it is possible to receive "dying grace." I encourage you to read up on it quickly before going further as it is a fortunate opportunity that I believe was given to my father. Dying grace means simply, the chance to see both sides of life, the here and eternity. My father was not the only one to experience this phenomenon, nor will he be the last. If you are in a season of life where you're helping your loved one transition from this world, listen to them. The glimpses into this new realm are genuinely an incredible gift to behold and be told.

My father knew I was listening to every word he said, and almost taking notes. At one point, he'd said, "I probably shouldn't be telling you this. I should be quiet before I get in trouble. Somethings you aren't supposed to know yet." But now that I know, should I keep it a secret?

Many times, throughout the Bible, Jesus asked those he helped to keep the miracles he performed a secret. This request was often an effort by Jesus not to distract from the message he was teaching. By sharing with you, do I worry that I am making an eternal mistake? Quite the opposite. The statement "Make known among the nations what he has done," can be found in more than one location in the Bible. I am confident I was supposed to share this.

.

Chapter 11: Going Home

"Jesus called out with a loud voice,
"Father, into your hands I commit my spirit."
When he said this, he breathed his last."
Luke 23:46 New International Version (NIV)

We made the decision that my father was going to come home. Hospice had helped prepare the necessary equipment in his room beside my mother, just as it should be. It is where he'd always said he wanted to be when he took his last breath.

The hour before he left the hospital was emotional. The majority of his days, he had been cared for by the same nurse. Although she was saddened by his decision to go home and cease further treatment, she understood that it was his wish to no longer go through the painful procedures that were likely of no help. In the few weeks my father had been there, he'd touched her heart as well.

My father showed excitement about the transfer from the hospital to his own home. It was painful, and many times I was worried that the pain would be too great to overcome. However, his spirit carried him through. Being in his room would prove to be just what he needed.

On July 25th, 2018, my father returned home to sleep beside his wife in his room. He was alert, smiling, and full of jokes. My dad looked forward to meeting the new nurse assigned to his home care. My uncle bought an electric razor and proceeded to wash and shave his face lovingly. Although he hadn't eaten in days, he suddenly had an appetite.

The family gathered around as he enjoyed a few bites of yogurt and sipped some water. Things began to look up, if even for just a little while. We all sat with him individually and enjoyed talking and basking in my father's light of love. It was a good day and gave us a renewed hope for what being home would look like.

Later in the day, we met with the hospice people. They asked us an interesting question. They asked if my father knew *why* he was home. I think we had all assumed that he was coherent enough of the conversations in the hospital that he understood.

As nighttime approached, and I was readying to leave my parent's home for the day, I went in to tell my father good night. Something inside me told me I should ask my father if he knew why we'd brought him home.

Lovingly I hugged my father, and I asked, "Dad, do you know *why* we brought you home from the hospital? Your nurse that's helping mom thinks we should make sure you know *why* we brought you home."

My father replied, "Well yeah! Because you want me to die!"

Flabbergasted, my mouth dropped open in disbelief. Did my father really believe we'd removed him from the consistent care of the hospital to drag him home out of mere convenience? I was hurt and, at the same time, resolute in the hope that my father understood that we had done this all out of love.

"Don't be ridiculous, Dad!" I'd said. "No one wants you to die."

Then, with tears in my eyes, I replayed the last few months to him; how the cancer had returned and spread to other parts of his body. I asked him if he remembered how they'd asked to do an MRI of his brain, and other tests, which he'd refused.

When he said that he remembered, I told him that if he wanted to return to the hospital and give it a go, we'd call them and send him back right now. He looked at me and said, "It won't do any good. The cancer is too bad. I won't survive any more tests or procedures. I can't. My body can't."

I told him that's why we brought him home so that he could be comfortable with no more tests, no more procedures, just us. Just home. Just love.

To this, he replied, "Oh, now I guess I do understand God!"

On the morning of July 26th, 2018, my father woke and was talking leisurely with my mother and me when an alarm went off on his phone.

"What is that sound?" he asked.

"I believe that's your phone," my mother had replied. "You had an alarm set because today is your grandson's birthday. He is twenty today."

"Oh, no!" my father said with a gasp. "It is his birthday? I didn't know that was today. Oh no! No, no, no!"

"What is it?" I asked.

"Well, I need to have a talk here. Okay? I mean, I have to do this really quick," my father said. "Just hold on," then he closed his eyes.

"God, we need to change the plan," he spoke as if praying.

My mother and I looked at each other in disbelief and smiled.

Then, as if holding a conversation with someone, my father responded with "yes" and "mm-hmm" a few times. Finally, as if finishing his discussion, he said, "Okay, Lord, okay. That will work. Thank you, God." When he opened his eyes, he looked at us and smiled.

"What was that?" I asked him.

"Had to change the plan," he responded thoughtfully with a quirky raise of his eyebrows.

"You did, huh?" I asked.

"Yep, it's okay now, though. God said it was okay," he stated.

"Well, that's good," my mother responded. "I'm glad you got that worked out."

He looked at my mother and said, "Yeah, me too. Not today, today would not have been a good day for what we had planned."

That day carried on with my father spending less and less time talking and more and more time sleeping. When he was awake, many of us would just sit, smiling, and holding his hand while he smiled back. Sometimes it seemed he was not always quite there. He'd quit drinking fluids and hadn't asked for food. I sat with him and wet his lips with water from a sponge and rubbed his hands with lotion. It seemed he needed rest, and so individually, we would go in and sit with him for the periods he appeared to be awake.

Later that evening, I heard him speaking with his brother. He was reviewing the names of his brother's grandchildren. They went through a long list of relatives, who had children, and what their names were now. It seemed he was putting together a family tree of sorts. After its completion, he appeared tired, and my uncle left the room.

A while later, my father woke again. I heard him asking if his brother was still there. I replied that he was and called for my uncle to come back. My father looked at my uncle and stated, "You're Don Trembly."

"Yes, I am," replied my uncle.

My father smiled, closed his eyes, and said, "And I'm Delford Trembly."

My Uncle chuckled, and said, "Yes, you are Delford Trembly. You are my brother."

Those were the last words I would hear my father speak. His recounting of the family names and various branches of the tree may seem unusual, but as time has gone on, I have come to realize that it is beautiful. During his last days, he'd asked about certain people and their last names. He always closed his eyes afterward, in prayer. He was asking about the people that he loved so that he could pray for them individually. Even those he hadn't seen in such a long time, those he barely knew; he was praying for them by name.

July 27th, 2018 began with the rising of the sun as with any other day. However, having known about the conversation my father had the day before, my mother and I were a bit uneasy.

My father's condition had gotten worse. Before leaving for the weekend, the hospice nurse told us that his prognosis was not good; the end was near.

As it would be for a woman married nearly forty-nine years, my mother was struggling. She struggled to accept what was happening, while dually trying to stay awake and be strong. Since my father was no longer speaking, she worried he was hurting and was unable to let us know. My mother confessed that although my father didn't like the taste of the pain medicine, she had deceived him by claiming it helped him to breathe better.

As the day passed, my father wouldn't open his eyes. I believed he was awake and alert, but he just couldn't open his eyes anymore. He barely moved at all. Worried, my mother asked him to wiggle his eyebrows if he wanted the medicine that made him breathe better. My father responded by raising his eyebrows just a bit. Without hesitation, my mother dashed to the kitchen to retrieve the pain medicine.

With my mother out of the room, and my father seemingly completely aware, he slowly turned his head and looked at me. Shocked that he'd moved even a little bit, I looked down to see what important thing he needed only to see my father looking up at me and rolling his eyes! He was trying to be funny!

Right then, right during the middle of it all, he'd rolled his eyes at my mother behind her back. It was a classic, dad move on his part. Though he'd not spoken a word, he'd all but said, "Oh my goodness, the lengths your mother won't go through to make sure she's taking care of me." Even at that moment, without words, he said it so well.

Oh, how I laughed! "You're rotten, Dad! Don't do that! You stinker! You're going to get in trouble," I warned him. When my mother returned with the medicine, he opened his mouth just enough to ingest it. Then he followed with a small, mischievous smirk planted across his lips. Oh, how I loved his sense of humor.

As night came, and the day was gone, I realized my time had run out. I didn't want to leave. It was my last day with my father. I knew that night when I left, I would never see him again in this life. I struggled to make my body move to leave the room as a result, and I realized I was keeping my mother awake. She didn't want to disturb my time with Dad, but she truly needed her rest. I realized my selfishness at that moment, and I gave in to the fact that I had to leave.

In tears, I leaned over my father. I reminded him of how good he was, and I praised him for his love and kindness in this life. I reminded him all that he'd shown me, and countless others, would not be forgotten. Quite simply, I told him he was the best, and I was so fortunate God chose him to be my father. Then I asked him to remember me when it was my time to go to where he was going. I told him I would know it was time, and safe to go, when he came for me just as Violet had come for him. I told him how very much I loved him and how I would see him soon. As I sat back up to leave, I looked down to see my father's face one final time.

As his daughter, I knew what my father looked like the few times in my life that I'd seen him cry. At that moment, unable to open his eyes, I knew my father 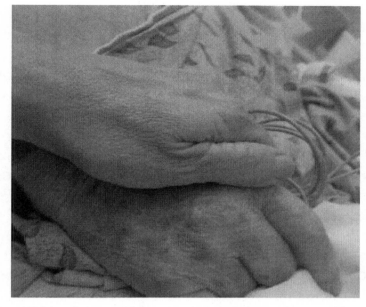 was crying. I told him I loved him again and forced myself to leave his room. Just outside, I hugged my mom and told her good night. I told her to get some rest and headed home.

When my phone rang in the middle of the night, I knew before I answered. My father was no longer a part of this world. My mother couldn't speak at first. I could only hear her trying to keep from crying. "Is it time?" I asked her, to which she was barely able to whisper, "Yes, it's time. He's gone."

In the early morning hours of July 28th, 2018, just as my father had said it would be, he took his last breath. It was not on my son's birthday, just as my father said it wouldn't be. It was the time of his choosing, just as the Bible says it can be.

I believe my father chose when he would commit his spirit into God's hands. Certain events had to happen; certain people had to be there, while certain others needed to be absent before he could leave this world.

God gives us free will. If you live your life to its completion with His purpose as your goal, do you not think He will let you choose the hour you commit your spirit back into His hands?

I'm so blessed to have spent my father's final days with him. I'm even more thankful that someone told me to listen to him, and not disregard his ramblings as side effects of medicine, or loss of reason. Even in the days before his death, my father was sharing and teaching.

Just as he had predicted, when his light left this world, everything changed.

I feel like he handed off his magnificent torch and said, "Here, child. You heard me. You carry it."

Proudly, I will.

Epilogue

"Blessed are you when people insult you, persecute you and falsely say all kinds of evil against you because of me." Matthew 5: 11 New International Version (NIV)

𝒯he following is what I wrote and read at my father's memorial service.

"One of Dad's favorite songs by Casting Crowns begins:
"Who am I, that the Lord of all the earth
Would care to know my name
Would care to feel my hurt?"

He felt so blessed in this life because he knew the Lord.

The Lord knew his name; felt his hurt.

He felt he had been given so much by God, and that it was his responsibility to share what he had with others who had less.

My Dad's kind of sharing wasn't always being "generous" with money. To him, sharing was also encouragement, caring, kindness, love, his time, and sharing his faith.

My Father was just trying to be Christ-like.

He believed he was always a work in progress, even in his final days.

If you are sitting here today, chances are good, in some way, my Dad shared something, some feeling, with you.

You most likely have a little piece of him with you, just like we do... Just like I do.

Many of you recently have told me how my Father made a difference to you. I've heard he was "such a beautiful man," "so positive," "such a big heart."

Do you know why he was all of those things?

I believe this quote I heard from author Marianne Williamson sums up my father's message.

I'm going to read it to you, and as you listen, I just want you to imagine my Dad. I believe this is what he was always trying to share with all of us:

"Our deepest fear is not that we are inadequate.
Our deepest fear is that we are powerful beyond
measure.
It is our light, not our darkness,
that most frightens us.
We ask ourselves,
'Who am I to be brilliant, gorgeous, talented,
fabulous?'
Actually, who are you not to be?
You are a child of God.
Your playing small does not serve the world.
There is nothing enlightened about shrinking so that
other people won't feel insecure around you.
We are all meant to shine as children do.
We were born to make manifest
the glory of God that is within us.
It's not just in some of us; it's in everyone.
And as we let our own light shine, we unconsciously
give other people permission to do the same.
As we are liberated from our own fear,
our presence automatically liberates others."
— Marianne Williamson, A Return to Love:
Reflections on the Principles of "A Course in Miracles"

So that's what he did.

He let go of feeling small, and he wasn't afraid of being empowered. He quit believing he wasn't good enough, and he mastered letting his light shine, and then…

He gave you permission to do and be the same.

With many of you, in the time he spent with you, in his presence, you felt more positive, more encouraged, happier, loved; he gave you hope.

It's because he was giving you permission to shine!

He never tried to tell you who he thought you should be. He just tried to help you become the best person you could be... who he believed you could be.

He never tried to put your light out, he just tried to help you shine.

Who are we to not be the people my father believed us to be?

We can't just stop now because he's gone...

Who would I be, not to carry on his light? That would be the biggest disappointment to my dad.

So, when you leave here today, go and be the people my father was excited to call his friends, his family, the people he left his light with.

Forgive and go. Love each other; forever and always.

Go on from here today, be empowered, build each other up, and let your own light shine, just like my Dad would have wanted you to."

People came that day to share stories of the light he had been within their lives. Friends that I had never known expressed their gratitude and gathered in the love that my father fostered within their lives.

So, maybe you think I'm crazy; maybe I'm not. Perhaps you think my dad was. However, I don't believe that to be true. I think my dad had it right. He was always waiting for the rest of us to figure it out.

There is a scientific theory that suggests "Dimethyltryptamine," or DMT is released just before a person dies. The theory suggests that this psychedelic molecule is the reason for near-death experiences, only released at the time of birth, death, or extreme stress. The scientific community uses this theory as a reason to explain away experiences by believers when they are suggesting angels are present, or that they have met Jesus, etc.; however, it is *just* a theory. At this time, the claim is not substantiated.

Let's assume the scientists are onto something. The molecule found in plants, and in trace amounts in people, would be needed in large quantities to create such dream-like experiences. Let's assume it really is available at times of birth, death, and extreme stress, just as they suggest.

How did it get there? It is known our bodies have the molecule in trace amounts in our blood, urine, and spinal fluid. There is speculation it is in the pituitary gland, waiting for release at the beginning and the end of life. If so, how do you explain its release, the timing of the release, the amount, the triggering factor? The theory has many unknowns.

What if the molecule is necessary? What if God placed it there so that, upon the beginning or end of life, he can more closely communicate with us? What if it's needed to open up our minds and our hearts to listen for His voice more closely? What if it's required to open up our eyes to see, even when they are closed?

Science will always try to win the battle.

My father was always one to say, "What harm will come if you live your life as if this is not the end, and what you do in this life matters? If you live your life in that way, then you will always be right."

May this book speak to your heart, and shine light into your darkness. May it bring you hope and joy.

Please let me know if this book has made a difference to you. I would love to hear your story.

Email me at butdidyoushine@gmail.com.

I will send you* a complimentary mini E-book, "Shine On!" when I receive your email. It continues where this story left off, proving God is always working for our good.

Thank you for reading. Now go on… Shine!

(*Complimentary E-book will be sent via digital download after 7/28/2021)

About the Author

Kimberly Trembly-Carr was born in rural Nebraska and moved to the Phoenix metropolitan area in 1985. She met her husband, Travis, in 2009. She has 3 boys of her own, including a set of twins. She is active in her community, she helps manage her husband's business, and she is a licensed real estate agent. She enjoys spending time with family (especially at the lake), photography, and reading.

Made in the USA
San Bernardino, CA
30 June 2020